KT-366-454

INITIATION
AND EUCHARIST
Essays on their Structure

BY THE JOINT LITURGICAL GROUP

EDITED BY
Neville Clark and Ronald C. D. Jasper

LONDON SPCK

First published in 1972
Second impression 1973
by S.P.C.K.
Holy Trinity Church
Marylebone Road
London NW1 4DU

Printed in Great Britain by
William Clowes & Sons, Limited
London, Beccles and Colchester

SBN 281 02735 8

CONTENTS

THE JOINT LITURGICAL GROUP

MEMBERS

1 *Church of England*
The Dean of Bristol (the Very Reverend D. E. W. Harrison), *Chairman*
The Reverend D. C. Gray
The Reverend Canon R. C. D. Jasper, *Secretary*

2 *Church of Scotland*
The Reverend Dr R. S. Louden
F. N. Davidson Kelly, Esq.

3 *The Baptist Union of Great Britain and Ireland*
The Reverend N. Clark
The Reverend S. F. Winward

4 *The Congregational Church in England and Wales*[1]
The Reverend W. E. Evans
The Reverend J. M. Todd

5 *The Episcopal Church in Scotland*
The Reverend Canon A. O. Barkway
The Reverend Canon E. W. Brady

6 *The Methodist Church*
The Reverend A. R. George
The Reverend G. S. Wakefield

7 *The Presbyterian Church of England*[1]
The Reverend R. A. Davies
The Reverend W. N. Leak

8 *The Churches of Christ*
The Reverend Dr W. G. Baker

9 *The Roman Catholic Church*
Mgr G. A. Tomlinson
The Reverend H. Winstone

[1] In October 1972 these two bodies united to become the United Reformed Church.

STATEMENT OF 11 OCTOBER 1963

Informal discussions on liturgical matters between interested people from various Churches in Great Britain have indicated that the time is now ripe for the creation of a Joint Liturgical Group which can develop given projects and questions of public worship. The Archbishop of Canterbury was asked to help bring such a Group into being by issuing invitations to the Churches concerned to appoint members. His Grace kindly agreed to do so and himself appointed the representatives of the Church of England, while those of other Churches have been appointed by their respective bodies.

At its first meeting on 10–11 October 1963 the Group elected the Dean of Bristol as its Chairman and Dr Jasper as its Secretary.

It is clearly to be understood that any work produced by this Group will have no authority greater than that which its own members give to it by their own weight; but it will be for particular Churches, through their customary modes of decision, to make use of the results if they are willing to do so.

The initial projects which the Group has decided to discuss are these:

1. The planning of a Calendar, Forms of Daily Service, and a Lectionary which the Churches might be glad to have in common.

2. The planning of joint forms of service which might be used with the approval of the several Churches on occasions for united worship, such as the Week of Prayer for Unity and Holy Week.

3. The consideration of the structure of the service of Holy Communion.

GENERAL INTRODUCTION

In presenting this work to the Churches for their consideration, it is important to emphasize that it is modest in aim and limited in scope. We are simply attempting to suggest the direction in which progress might be made, and to offer a provisional sketch map of the terrain that might be occupied. Is there sufficient theological agreement to make possible the increasing adoption of recognizably common structures for the Eucharist and Initiation ? This is the crucial question that is posed.

In 1968 the World Council of Churches drew up a statement on *The Eucharist in Ecumenical Thought* which brought together agreements registered at Faith and Order Conferences since 1952. In 1971 a further report on *Ecumenical Agreement on Baptism* collated agreements similarly registered over the years from 1927. In addition the British Council of Churches has laid before the Churches of this country a Certificate of Christian Baptism which, if accepted, would advance mutual recognition of their baptismal rites. Such facts may serve to indicate that theological consensus is not entirely lacking.

Yet in what follows no attempt is made to state and argue total theological positions which might be universally acceptable. To embark on such a task would demand extensive discussion, the quoting of authorities, the refuting of positions, the weighing of a vast mass of evidence. It would almost certainly lead at some point to an impasse. It would probably distract attention from the main concern.

It will be for others to argue whether the basis of common understanding which is made explicit here provides an acceptable and sufficient foundation for the common structures which are worked out and commended.

THE STRUCTURE OF CHRISTIAN INITIATION

Ecumenical developments in recent years have made the search for an agreement on the basic issues of Christian initiation increasingly more necessary. At the same time, pastoral perplexity and anxiety about traditional practices have deepened. Contemporary pressures pose old questions with a new urgency.

The Faith and Order Commission of the World Council of Churches registered a measure of ecumenical consensus on the meaning of baptism in *One Lord, One Baptism* (1960). The last decade has, however, witnessed no further theological advance, and has arguably been marked by a certain theological weariness. From 1967, WCC study has concentrated on considerations of liturgy and practice under the title *Baptism, Confirmation, and the Eucharist*.

Similar concerns have been reflected on the national scene. The thrust of the Nottingham Conference of 1964 was calculated to stimulate practical advances and programmes for action rather than leisurely theological reflections. In 1970 the British Council of Churches published its *Report of the Inter-Church Enquiry into Baptismal Practice*. The most recent and considerable statement on Christian Initiation, emanating in 1971 from the Church of England, was significantly subtitled *Birth and Growth in the Christian Society*.

When, in 1969, the Joint Study Group of Representatives of the Roman Catholic and Scottish Episcopal Churches produced a statement on *The Nature of Baptism and its Place in the Life of the Church*, it concluded with this plea: 'It would be fitting if the sacramental unity which we share through Baptism were expressed liturgically in a Rite of Baptism incorporating as far as possible a common ritual in a common text . . .' The report to the British Council of Churches in 1968 on *Areas of Ecumenical Experiment* was even more pointed. Recommendation 9 read: 'That the Joint Liturgical Group be asked to draw up an agreed form of service for Baptism as a basis for further discussion.' Clearly, the demand for common texts grows steadily.

At this point it may be of critical importance to keep our sights clear. Two dangers may have to be reckoned with and avoided. The one would be to halt all action on the search for and production of a common rite on the plea that any advance is impossible unless theological agreement at all points is first secured. The other would be to labour over texts which might pretend ecumenical acceptability only by reflecting attenuated theological foundations or by papering over the theological divides with ambiguous phraseology.

The way forward may become clearer if attention is paid to distinctions that emerge in connection with the understanding of the Church. There is the *faith* of the Church. There is the *order* of the Church. There is the *organization* of the Church. Order must express and be controlled by faith. It must be theologically grounded, so that the Church is ordered by the gospel. Order is the embodiment of a Church subject to the will of its Lord.

In the realm of organization no unvarying uniformity is necessarily demanded or desirable. Organization may be rightly affected by everything from traditional inheritance and national custom to the requirements of efficiency and the exigencies of the secular climate. Many organizational costumes are acceptable, provided that they do not contradict the common ordering of the Body.

So, it may be, with Christian initiation. The primary concern must be with common order, theologically rooted. Two conclusions follow. On the one hand, the search becomes one for agreement on liturgical structure rather than total uniformity of ritual and practice. On the other hand, the structure to be sought must be sufficiently and faithfully expressive of common theological understanding.

One further limitation of aim must be noted. A variety of rites, concerned with 'blessing' or 'naming' or 'admission to the catechumenate' or 'commissioning of adults', marks the contemporary scene. None is unimportant. All require careful consideration. The immediate and specific preoccupation here is, however, something different and distinguishable. It is nothing less and nothing other than the substance of Christian initiation.

So the ground is staked out and the goal made plain. It remains to be asked whether the hope of moving towards a common structure is a realistic one, or whether the depth of the theological differences renders advance impracticable. It is certain that deep differences of conviction remain, not least in the matter of whether it is the baptism of infants or the baptism of believers that must be adjudged to be normative.

The continuing chasms must not be concealed. Yet it is not wholly clear that progress towards a common structure of Christian initiation must wait upon the resolution of all such differences. The traffic is not completely one-way. It may be that the acceptance and use of an agreed framework might open fresh possibilities of reaching a more adequate common understanding.

To say that is not to deny that structure must reflect theology. A common structure indeed demands for its undergirding a firm theological base. But the crucial question is whether such significant differences of conviction as at present exist can properly and for the time being be contained within an overarching theological understanding. It may be that the measure of theological agreement already widely present is sufficient to make a fuller measure of common structure possible.

It is important that the wide mutual recognition of baptism across denominational frontiers—in terms of the use of water and the trinitarian formula—should not be jeopardized. It is, however, equally important that the attempt to build some fuller agreement upon this minimal base should not be abandoned. What follows is offered as a contribution to the ongoing task.

A. THE TOTAL BAPTISMAL REALITY

1. Baptism is not simply to be understood as a rite, administered at some limited and particular point in time. Understood in a fully biblical context it refers to an act behind which stands a depth of meaning and significance relating to divine action. To speak of baptism is indeed to speak of the appointed *act* of Christian initiation. But it is also, and at the same time, and more importantly, to speak of a *complex meaning* visibly focused in sacramental action. Certainly, act and meaning, sign and significance, are not to be separated. But equally certainly, consideration of the total baptismal reality must precede judgements about the baptismal rite.

2. Baptism (in this total biblical sense) is sacrament of redemption. Yet redemption itself must be understood from scriptural perspective. It comprehends the whole range and reach of the biblical story. It is bounded only by creation and consummation—finding its focus and control in the action of God in Jesus Christ. Thus redemption cannot be explicated as a *momentary* reality. It is to be understood in terms of all three tenses, past, present, and future. As sacrament of redemption, the same holds true for baptism. The whole meaning and effect of the baptismal rite itself cannot therefore be tied to the moment of its performance.

3. Baptism must then be comprehended in terms of the redemptive action of God, and the understanding of it must be worked out from the christological centre. Certain things follow:

(*a*) Redemption is both past and future event. At the cross and resurrection redemption has been effected: at the *parousia* it will be brought to completion. So the Kingdom has come, yet awaits its full manifestation. So the Spirit has been given, yet remains in us the first-fruits of the inheritance. So the Church is the Body of Christ, yet remains under the Cross. So the Christian has been justified, yet awaits final salvation.

Baptism is thus a sacrament of inaugurated eschatology. It is grounded in the atoning work of Christ which it applies and extends. It looks towards the *parousia*. No temporal moment can therefore comprehend its fullness. The basic concern must then be that all essential elements find ritual expression. Whether they must be expressed at one time becomes an important but strictly secondary issue.

(*b*) The redemptive action of God is focused in the death and resurrection of Jesus Christ. Baptism is into Christ: and to be 'in Christ' is to enter into the new birth, to be regenerate. It is to share his death and resurrection, to die to sin and to rise to newness of life. The dying to sin comprehends a turning from the old, focused in cleansing and forgiveness. The rising to newness of life comprehends a turning to God, focused in the gift of the Spirit.

Therefore the baptismal rite must make plain this decisive movement and passage from sin through death to new life.

(*c*) The transition from the old order to the new is based upon communion with Christ, in whom God's covenantal dealing with his People comes to fulfilment. Such relationship to Christ involves faith. The baptismal union is a faith union. This faith is not an autonomous human contribution standing over against God's grace in some complementary fashion. It is the displacement of man's illusory liberty by the faithfulness of Christ. It is that responsible human decision which is evoked and made possible by the divine gift and summons.

Therefore the pattern of divine address and human response, of grace and faith, must mark the baptismal rite.

(d) To be engrafted into Christ is to be incorporated into the *totus Christus*. It is to be initiated into the Body of Christ. But the Church is the representation in servant guise of the Kingdom of God. It is the bridgehead of the Kingdom's victory, at once the representation and the servant of what at last will be. It lives between the cross/resurrection and the *parousia*.

So baptism is initiation into the People of God who recognize Christ's finished work, acknowledge his present lordship, and look to his final victory. As such, it is 'ordination' to the priestly Body of Christ sent on mission to the world. The initiatory rite must visibly express commissioning and empowering to that end.

Such a theological understanding of the total baptismal reality makes plain the profound significance of Christian initiation. It is the sacrament of incorporation into the Spirit-filled Body of Christ. Specifically it emerges as:

   sacrament of inaugurated eschatology
   sacrament of rebirth by union with Christ through death and
      resurrection
   sacrament of empowering for the corporate ministry of the royal
      priesthood, the People of God

Accordingly, these notes must find expression in the initiatory rite.

B. THE TOTAL RITE OF
CHRISTIAN INITIATION

1. In traditional terms, the total rite of Christian initiation might be described as baptism, confirmation, and first communion. But

such usage is not in all respects either self-explanatory or entirely happy.

(a) In the first place, there is the suggestion of three quite distinct and separable acts. Thus does accidental historical development blur the theological realities.

(b) In the second place, 'confirmation' is an ambiguous term which too easily obscures the truth that the eucharist is the necessary and proper confirmation of baptism. It will therefore be clearer at this point to speak of anointing with oil (chrism) and/or the laying on of hands.

2. The total process and progression of Christian initiation, then, extends from the washing with water to the sharing of the bread and wine. It is baptism reaching its conclusion in eucharist. And the initiatory rite itself is washing in water associated (by long tradition) with anointing with chrism and/or the laying on of hands.

3. The various aspects of meaning which belong to the initiatory reality have already been noted. These are rightly and specially to be borne in mind in connection with the various elements of the initiatory rite. Thus we properly and appropriately associate washing in water with inaugurated eschatology and union through death and resurrection, and anointing/laying on of hands with empowering. Yet the total significance of the initiatory reality must not, in any final sense, be segmented. For such segmentation presses inexorably towards a falsely instantaneous view of sacramental action that suggests that different things are 'effected' at different moments.

C. THE LITURGICAL EXPRESSION OF CHRISTIAN INITIATION

Certain controlling principles may be enunciated. As sacrament of Christian initiation, the rite belongs within the Liturgy of the Church, within that service of Word and Sacrament which concerns the baptized and the catechumens. It is thus surrounded necessarily and *de facto* by the faith of the Church.

Within this Liturgy the proper placing of the rite is at the hinge of Word and Supper. Such a conclusion is not accidental. The rite stems from the Word proclaimed and moves towards the Supper.

Further, while diversity of 'use' is rightly and fully to be allowed for, it is nevertheless desirable that the essential structure should not be overladen or obscured. From this perspective it may be questioned how far the traditional multiplicity of words is any longer helpful. Much speaking is not necessarily the index of importance and solemnity.

The basic pattern and progression would seem to be as follows:

1. *The Scriptural Warrant*

The thrust of the New Testament in general and the understanding of the Gospel writers in particular support the conclusion that Christian baptism rests upon and stems from the baptism of Jesus at Jordan taken to its fulfilment in his Cross. It is the passing of the Jordan baptism through the cross and the resurrection that produces and makes possible Christian baptism. This suggests that the appropriate words of scripture are Mark 1.9–11, Matt. 28.18–20, and Acts 2.38.

A form such as the following might therefore be proposed.

At the beginning of his earthly ministry, our Lord received baptism at the hands of John. At the cross his baptism found fulfilment. Beyond the resurrection the Holy Spirit was given to the Church, and the Apostle Peter called the people to Christian baptism. Hear the words of scripture, recorded in the Gospel according to St Mark, the Gospel according to St Matthew, and the Acts of the Apostles:

In those days Jesus came from Nazareth of Galilee and was baptized by John in the Jordan. And when he came up out of the water, immediately he saw the heavens opened and the Spirit descending upon him like a dove; and a voice came from heaven, 'Thou art my beloved Son; with thee I am well pleased.'

And Jesus came and said to them, 'All authority in heaven and on earth has been given to me. Go therefore and make disciples of all nations, baptizing them in the name of the Father and of the Son and of the Holy Spirit, teaching them to observe all that I have commanded you; and lo, I am with you always, to the close of the age.'

And Peter said to them, 'Repent and be baptized every one of you in the name of Jesus Christ for the forgiveness of your sins; and you shall receive the gift of the Holy Spirit.'

Christian baptism is thus the visible sign and seal of that new relationship to God opened to men by the cross and resurrection. By this sacrament we are solemnly admitted into the Church of Christ and engaged to be his. Here God meets us in claim and in promise. Here he assures to us the gift of the Holy Spirit and our adoption in Christ as sons and daughters of his Kingdom.

2. *The Act of Renunciation*
An act of renunciation is traditional, fitting, and significant. If used, it belongs at this point, prior to the Prayer. The candidate should be asked to signify that he repents of his sins, renounces evil, and turns to Christ.

3. *The Prayer at the Font or Baptistry*
A rehearsal of the 'mighty acts' of God belongs to the substance of this prayer. But the rite is performed in the context of the whole Liturgy, and the mighty acts will be celebrated at the heart of the eucharistic prayer. The reference at this point may therefore be brief.

The prayer should then move to petition that God will so be present in the power of the Spirit, so use this water of baptism, so work in and through the sacramental action, with regard to those to be baptized, that:

delivered from the dominion of sin they may be reborn into the freedom of the children of God

buried with Christ they may rise with him to newness of life

baptized into the one Body they may share in the one Spirit.

4. *The Act of Baptism*
The congregation of the baptized should here stand, in solemn token of the shared solidarity of faith, and in acceptance of responsibility in the continuing nurture of those to be baptized.

Since the baptismal union is a faith union, an act of faith should stand in immediate relationship to the washing in water. It will include elements of profession and commitment. The use of the Apostles' Creed interrogatively is an obvious possibility. An alternative form might be of this nature:

Q Do you confess the Christian faith as set forth in Holy Scripture, committing yourself

in worship to the one God, the Father your Creator, the Son your Saviour, the Spirit your Helper
in fellowship to the one Church of Christ
in love and service to all men?

A I do.

Baptism should then be administered.

N, I baptize you in the Name of the Father and of the Son and of the Holy Spirit.

5. *The Laying on of Hands/Anointing with Chrism*
This traditional part of the initiatory rite fittingly includes the following:

(*a*) A questioning of the candidate in some such form as

Q Do you resolve to make diligent use of the means of grace, the Word, the Sacrament, and Prayer, and thus depending upon God and gratefully accepting the good things that are ours in Christ, to live the life of witness and obedience, and to work and pray for the coming of the Kingdom?

A I do.

(*b*) A prayer—that to this end God may empower by his Spirit . . .

(*c*) The act of Laying on of Hands/Anointing
N, the Lord empower you for service by his Spirit.

(If there is only one candidate the prayer (*b*) and the laying on of hands/anointing (*c*) would be one act.)

Here the Liturgy should resume with the Intercessions.

D. THE TOTAL RITE DIVIDED

It has been necessary to consider first the complete process of initiation, since it is only in the light of the total act in its wholeness that proper judgements about the various elements within it can be made. Clearly, however, in the common practice of the Church, Christian initiation is not performed in its entirety at one time. At this point, the considerations that should control require careful statement. Three may be offered.

The structure of the total rite should be minimally varied.

The association of sign with what is signified should be closely preserved.

The eschatological nature of the sacrament, and the consequent impossibility of confining its total meaning and reality to any moment or moments in time, should be frankly admitted.

Such considerations would seem both to allow and yet to set limits to the variation of the total pattern already outlined. The conclusions that emerge are as follows:

(a) Any disturbance of the *progression* 'Washing in water—laying on of hands/anointing with chrism—first communion' should generally be avoided as being destructive of the meaning of the rite. The washing in water and the laying on of hands/anointing with chrism belong to a total initiatory process which finds its sealing and completion in first communion.

(b) Both the washing in water and the laying on of hands/anointing with chrism should fall within the Liturgy, at the hinge of Word and Supper.

(c) The personal renunciation and profession of faith should not be included in infant baptism.

1. *Infant Baptism*
The progression of this Service would then be:

(a) The Scriptural Warrant

(b) An Act of Confession and Commitment
In appropriate form, the parents should make confession of the

Faith, and express committal to the vocation of Christian parenthood—to the end that the child shall come to repent of sin, renounce evil, and turn to Christ.

(c) The Prayer at the Font or Baptistry

(d) The Act of Baptism

The congregation of the baptized should here stand, in solemn token of the shared solidarity of faith, and in acceptance of responsibility in the continuing nurture of those to be baptized.

Baptism should then be administered.

There should follow an appropriate affirmation, to the effect that the child is received into the fellowship of the one Church of Christ, placed under the promises of God, and set by his Spirit in the path of life.

(It should be noted that some Churches have, at this point, a laying on of hands and/or anointing with oil. This may, or may not—according to the intention of the particular rite—constitute the second stage of the process of initiation.)

Here the Liturgy should resume with the Intercessions—including prayer for the home.

2. *Laying on of Hands/Anointing with Chrism*

The progression of this service for those who can answer for themselves would then be:

(a) A Scriptural Statement

In the days of your infancy you were by baptism committed to the Body of Christ, and all the promises of God were sealed to you. Those promises he has performed. It is he who now brings you to renounce evil, to make profession of your faith, to consecrate yourself to his service, and in the power of his Spirit to enter into the fullness of your inheritance.

Hear then the scripture:

You are a chosen race, a royal priesthood, a holy nation, God's own people, that you may declare the wonderful deeds of him who called you out of darkness into his marvellous light (1 Peter 2.9).

(*b*) An Act of Renunciation, Faith, and Commitment

(The congregation of the baptized standing, in solemn token of the shared solidarity of penitence and faith, and in acceptance of responsibility in the continuing nurture of those to be 'confirmed'.)

This should involve a questioning of the candidate in some such form as

1. Q Do you repent of your sins, renounce evil, and turn to Christ?

   A I do.

2. The interrogative use of the Apostles' Creed or some appropriate alternative form.

3. Q Do you resolve to make diligent use of the means of grace, the Word, the Sacrament, and Prayer, and thus depending upon God and gratefully accepting the good things that are ours in Christ, to live the life of witness and obedience, and to work and pray for the coming of the Kingdom?

   A I do.

(*c*) A Prayer—that to this end God may empower by his Spirit . . .

(*d*) The Act of Laying on of Hands/Anointing with Chrism.

   N, the Lord empower you for service by his Spirit.

(If there is only one candidate the prayer (*c*) and the laying on of hands/anointing (d) would be one act.)

Here the Liturgy should resume with the Intercessions.

THE STRUCTURE OF
THE EUCHARIST

Christian worship is the beating heart of the Church's life. It is in liturgical assembly that the People of God is formed, renewed, and equipped for mission, as week by week she is set under the cross and resurrection of her Lord and summoned to recapitulate the strange journey from baptism through the Word to the Table and out once more into the teeming life of men.

It is in the eucharist that the inalienable unity of the Church is disclosed. Yet it is here that her existing divisions are most starkly revealed. The search for 'intercommunion' at one level reflects the instinctive understanding that here the stakes are highest, and everything is hazarded, lost, or won.

Theological problems remain. The quest for theological agreement continues and must continue. Progress in recent decades has been substantial, as old and divisive refrains have been transposed into a new and more ecumenically singable key. Of this transformation, the Anglican–Roman Catholic *Agreed Statement on Eucharistic Doctrine* (September 1971) is, on one front, the most recent sign.

Yet theological debate is not the only urgent requirement. What men believe and how they understand is bound up with what they do and how they do it. Unless any emerging consensus is translated into liturgical practice, it remains theoretic and largely inoperative. Unless a common pattern of basic worship increasingly captures Christian hearts and minds and forms Christian experience, preparation for unity is critically retarded.

As with Christian initiation, so with the Liturgy of the Church. A common structure must be theologically grounded, reflecting a common theological understanding. Yet separated Churches, moving towards a common structure of worship, might expect that, in the doing, unifying theological insights might impose themselves. Any attempt to smother diversity in the name of uniformity would be indefensible. Yet to fail to express whatever emerging consensus of understanding may be glimpsed might be culpable disobedience.

The immediate concern may be precisely delineated. Forms of Christian worship may be many and varied, reflecting the particular reasons for particular gatherings of Christian people in the presence of God. But the heart of the worship of the Church is to be found in that liturgical assembly of the Lord's Day when the Family of God is called together to be remade the Body of Christ. This is the Liturgy of the Baptized, of those who have been initiated into the Body. Others may or may not be present, but this does not affect the essential purpose and structure of what is to be done.

It is in the belief that the existing measure of common understanding makes some form of common structure possible that this unfolding of the Liturgy is offered.

THE ESSENTIAL LITURGY

The Liturgy is essentially the Liturgy of Word and Supper. The two realities are distinguishable, yet they belong together within an over-arching unity. Several factors have, however, tended to accentuate the division at the expense of the unity.

There is, first of all, the dual origin of the Liturgy—in Synaxis[1] and Lord's Supper. Whether, in earliest Christian practice, these almost invariably belonged together as one unified act of worship or whether they formed separate and separable observances remains a debated historical question. What is clear is that they are related to different Jewish backgrounds; and that while the Supper is grounded in a Jewish religious meal (possibly the Passover and certainly with Passover overtones), the form of the Synaxis stems from the scripture reading, psalmody, and prayers that marked synagogue worship.

There is, secondly, the historical distinction in the early Christian centuries between the Liturgy of the Catechumens and the Liturgy of the Faithful. Here a break in the total act of worship was signalized by the dismissal of the catechumens prior to the Prayers of the Faithful.

There is, thirdly, the appearance of various truncated rites in the period following the Reformation. This was due to the need for

[1] A Greek word meaning 'gathering' or 'assembly' which came to be applied to that part of the Liturgy concerned with the Ministry of the Word.

some provision of worship in situations where insistence on communicating attendance as a basic element in the celebration of the eucharist was confronted by continued lay reluctance for frequent Communion.

It is worthy of note that the line of demarcation has not been the same in all cases. In itself this may serve to suggest that in some sense the unity is primary, the distinction secondary. Today, it is the massive and indissoluble unity of Word and Supper that imposes itself and demands emphasis. It is within such unity that the proper distinctions are rightly preserved.

Such unity in distinction demands careful liturgical expression. Word and Supper are properly bound to each other by liturgical material which both acts as response to the Word and points towards the Supper. If such material is to 'join' rather than to 'separate', it must not be allowed to become disproportionate.

THE WORD OF GOD
This part of the Liturgy consists essentially of Scripture, Sermon, and Intercession.

1. *Scripture*
The Bible is the record of a Word spoken in the past which, by the working of the Spirit, may become a Word spoken in and to the present. It is the story of the travail of God with his people, which culminated in the coming of the Christ and set in motion the Church's mission. It is the living and governing tradition by which the Church is anchored, into which she continually enters, and to which she must again and again return. It is the unique witness to that drama of redemption of which the Liturgy is the contemporary celebration.

This means that, if the Bible is to be allowed truly to speak, both Old Testament and New Testament must normally be read. Psalms (or equivalent hymnody) may appropriately be used at this point as vehicles of praise. They may equally serve here as commentary on the scriptures read. Yet these facts do not justify the exclusion of the whole of the Psalter from Scripture Reading.

2. *Sermon*
The Word proclaimed in Scripture Reading is to be brought to

contemporary fulfilment in the Word proclaimed in preaching. For scripture is not simply a book to be read. It is first of all and most of all words once spoken and heard, and therefore to be spoken again and heard anew. It is a story told that clamours to be retold, to the end that the depths of each contemporary situation may be exposed and the hearers be impelled to the shattering realization that they are participants.

This means that at the main Sunday service there will be a sermon.

3. Intercession

The Word of God is a gift that carries with it demand. But it not only claims response. It also governs that response and seeks to direct what its terms shall be. It turns the Church towards the world and imposes an inescapable intercessory responsibility.

So the People of God responds to the Word proclaimed in the exercise of its priestly ministry of intercession for all mankind. This is not response only. The Church, thus caught up into intercession, bears the world with her as she approaches the Supper.

THE SUPPER

The necessary connection of the Lord's Supper and the Last Supper and yet the necessary distinction between them must be carefully observed. The Lord's Supper is the Last Supper passed through the cross and resurrection. The concern of the Church is to celebrate the Lord's Supper, not to repeat the Last Supper. Yet the conscious rooting of the Feast in the fellowship meals of the Ministry, and supremely in the Last Supper, expresses the basic continuity between the earthly Jesus and the risen Lord.

It has often been argued that at the heart of the Eucharist must lie the fourfold action—'He took . . . blessed (or gave thanks) . . . broke . . . gave'. But it must be remembered that Scripture records a sevenfold action—'he took the bread . . . blessed (or gave thanks) . . . broke . . . gave; he took the cup . . . blessed (or gave thanks) . . . gave'. This is the practice still widely observed by such bodies as the Baptists and the Churches of Christ. It must be recognized that if strict fidelity to scripture is determinative in these matters, then it is the sevenfold action that should be observed. (The action indeed becomes ninefold if the saying of the interpretative words is included.)

It may, however, be argued that once the whole eucharistic action is severed from its initial rooting in a communal meal, original practice has already been abandoned, and strict adherence to a sevenfold action becomes quite artificial. It may further be argued that a double 'blessing' is repetitive; and that the emphasis upon the maintenance of the sevenfold action can ally itself a little too easily with a view of the Lord's Supper as repetition of the Last Supper.

Such cautions seem well grounded. Yet it must be realized that they strike an equally damaging blow against any idea that the fourfold action is essential to the Supper. An argument from tradition would, in this matter, seem as artificial as the argument from Scripture has been judged to be. All this would suggest that it is a theological judgement that is required, which takes proper account of Scripture and tradition.

From such a theological perspective, the basic action is seen to be twofold. 'He blessed (or gave thanks) . . . and gave.' The 'taking' is a necessary if solemn prelude to the 'blessing'. The 'breaking' is a necessary practical prelude to the 'giving'—which is itself in order that a sharing may take place. *It is therefore Thanksgiving and Communion that constitute the essential pillars of the eucharist.*

1. Presentation and Taking

The Church 'provides', and *often* the people's representatives 'bring', so that the president may 'take' and set apart the bread and wine. This is not to be confused with the eucharistic offering or oblation which is made (*a*) by thanksgiving in the eucharistic prayer and (*b*) in deed at Communion—these being one in the mystery and wholeness of the eucharistic drama.

Yet this complex of action, rightly understood, stands forth as a significant part of the Liturgy. It is the hinge from Word to Supper. On the one hand, it is a response to the Word proclaimed, and as such rightly involves gifts of money as well as bread and wine. On the other hand, what is brought and set apart in its own measure makes the Supper possible. This God will transform. With this God will feed us, unworthy though we be.

2. Eucharistic Prayer

This great Prayer of Thanksgiving is rightly seen as the 'liturgy' of the president. Yet in what is here done the People of God is essentially involved, and a proper measure of responsive participation is highly desirable. The whole is rightly to be set in the context of praise, e.g. Sursum Corda and Sanctus.

Three possible elements of this Prayer, apart from its essential content, require consideration: intercessory material, specific thanksgivings, and the Words of Institution.

(a) Within the Prayer intercessory material has, by long tradition, found a place in some rites in what are known as the Diptychs. These, however, were not general intercessions, but were a specific reference to the living and departed in the Church of God. There is no justification for duplicating the Prayers of the Faithful at this point.

(b) When specific thanksgivings are deemed necessary, their placing in the Liturgy constitutes a problem. A case can be made for including them in the early part of the eucharistic prayer. It is true that there is to be borne in mind the difference between 'thanksgivings' and the rehearsal of the mighty acts of God. Yet it is also true that thanksgiving is most properly offered and understood in relation to those mighty acts. It would seem that, provided it is not of a trivial nature, such thanksgiving may properly fall within the eucharistic prayer. Beyond this, it is often appropriate that thankful remembrances should also find a place within the Intercessions.

(c) With regard to the placing of the Words of Institution, a case can be made in three directions.

They may be viewed as the narrative-charter of the Supper, determinative for the whole action. This would suggest their insertion before the action begins.

They may be viewed as part of the rehearsal of the mighty acts of God and as the warrant for the *anamnesis*. This would dictate their insertion in the first section of the eucharistic prayer.

They may be viewed as the 'word' background to Communion, in harmony with the New Testament record of the last Supper. This would indicate their insertion before the act of Communion.

There would seem to be no one mandatory place for them. Yet

clearly the Words of Institution must find a place within the context of the Supper in view of their controlling significance.

The basic elements and progression of the eucharistic prayer remain. They are:

> the proclamation and recital of the mighty acts of God in creation and redemption
>
> the *anamnesis* (memorial) with the bread and wine of the crucified and risen Lord 'until he come'
>
> the petition that, by the power of the Holy Spirit, what we do may be united to the perfect sacrifice of Christ and so accepted by God that in communion with our Lord we may receive the benefits of his passion and victory.

In the consideration of the introduction of other liturgical material, attention must be given to the importance of ensuring that the prayer is not overloaded, and that its central thrust is not obscured.

3. *Fraction and Communion*

Here no real problem arises. The Fraction is the significant manual act related to Communion. Bread must be broken before it can be shared. It was only by extension of meaning—though early and understandable—that the act came to carry a powerful message, speaking of the Church or the broken body of Jesus. It must, however, be noted that, in the best manuscript evidence, the word 'broken' does not occur in 1 Corinthians 11.24.

This part of the Liturgy, then, is seen as consisting essentially of the great Eucharistic Prayer together with the act of Communion in the context of the Words of Institution.

The normative structure of the total Liturgy therefore emerges as:

> Old Testament Reading
> New Testament Reading(s)
> Sermon
> Intercession
> The Thanksgiving
> The Communion.

THE CORPORATE PREPARATION
OF THE PEOPLE

The essential Liturgy begins with the Scripture Readings. No prior introduction is basically required. Yet the Liturgy exists to be a vehicle of worship. Throughout, proper weight must be given to pastoral considerations—and nowhere more so than at this point. It is pastoral wisdom to recognize that a modern congregation is not necessarily composed of prepared people dizzy with the wonders of grace. Some preparation is desirable. The elements of it might best be:

1. *Praise of God*

We come with our lives, our needs, our joys, our sorrows, our world. In praise and adoration, all this is set in the light of the God whom we worship.

2. *Confession*

Before the God who is presented to us, our own need and the world's predicament are revealed in their true reality. So confession and penitence are prompted and directed. We seek forgiveness, receive an assurance of pardon, and acknowledge anew our reconciliation applied in .baptism. Then, as the baptized and reconciled children of God, we can 'do the Liturgy'. Alternatively, confession might with equal point become one of the elements which follow the hearing of the Word of God.

THE DISMISSAL OF THE PEOPLE

The act of Communion concludes the Liturgy. Those who have shared in the 'blessing' of the Supper scarcely need a further 'blessing' pronounced upon them. The only important subsequent requirement is a brief Dismissal which makes explicit the whole thrust of the Liturgy by sending us forth to the life and work of the People of God. But a blessing becomes appropriate when there are present those who have not shared in Communion.

Certainly it is undesirable to end 'in a whirl of purifications and postscripts' (Ronald Knox). Probably the only additional material—prior to the Dismissal—that is at all appropriate would be a suitable hymn or prayer or perhaps the Nunc Dimittis.

OTHER LITURGICAL ELEMENTS

Certain familiar liturgical elements remain, and these demand attention.

1. *Psalmody and Hymnody*
In the setting of the Liturgy, material of this kind finds fundamental justification as, but only as, it serves a proper liturgical use.

(a) A suitable canticle or hymn provides a fitting act of praise at the beginning of the Preparation.

(b) Psalmody as vehicle of prayer and praise most appropriately belongs in the context of the Scripture Readings.

(c) Some corporate response to the Proclamation of the Word in its 'Sunday particularity' seems warranted. A suitable hymn, immediately after the Sermon, may fittingly provide for this.

(d) An appropriate hymn or psalm might be sung at the Presentation and/or after Communion.

2. *The Lord's Prayer*
Almost any placing of this can be justified, and almost any argument becomes a theological rationalization. As the crown and summation of Christian prayer it might conclude the Intercession. Interpreted with eucharistic reference it might come at the close of the eucharistic prayer, or immediately precede or follow Communion. As the prayer of the baptized, the prayer of the People of God, it might stand as the very first act of the Liturgy of the Baptized—constituting the hinge from the Preparation to the Proclamation of the Word.

In the making of a decision, the question of the whole balance and proportions of the Liturgy needs to be kept clearly in mind.

3. *The Collect for the Day* (or other similar prayer form).
If this is to be used, it belongs in the context of the Word proclaimed, whether prior to the Readings as the first prayer of the congregation 'collected' for worship or after the Sermon as the 'collecting' of the theme of the Word proclaimed.

4. *The Creed*
The recital of the mighty acts of God in the eucharistic prayer fulfils the necessary purpose of credal proclamation. The use of the

Creed is thus in no way essential, though it may have value as an act of corporate participation in a summation of the Faith partly declared in the Scripture Readings. If it is to be used, this should occur before the action of the Supper is begun.

5. *The Peace*
If this is to be used, whether as word or act, it will be in the context of the Supper. There is no invariable tradition as to its exact placing; and any theological argument for a particular position seems to smack of special pleading.

A POSSIBLE BASIC PATTERN

There is ample room for a diversity of 'use'. National and cultural setting may rightly be expected to have its effect. Uniformity is not to be prized. A variety of ceremonial may rightly be envisaged. Yet in the present situation in Britain everything suggests the over-whelming desirability of a simplicity of structure that will clearly reveal the essential pillars of the Liturgy. This surely implies:

1. That Word and Supper shall be seen to be one, and not be 'cemented' by such a mass of liturgical material that the effect will be to separate rather than to join.

2. That the inseparable relationship of the Scripture Readings to each other, and of both to the Sermon, shall not be obscured by intruding material.

3. That the inseparable relationship of Thanksgiving and Communion shall not be obscured by intruding material.

In the light of such conclusions, a possible basic pattern might be:

Act of Praise and Adoration

Act of Confession and Assurance of Pardon (this element may come here or after the Intercession)

Collect (this element may come after the Sermon)

Scripture Readings (OT and NT with psalmody if desired)

Sermon

Hymn of Response (or Collect)

Intercession

Presentation (with hymn/psalm if desired)

The Taking

The Thanksgiving (controlled by the Narrative of Institution)

    Sursum Corda
    Recital of the Mighty Acts of God and Sanctus
    Anamnesis
    Petition

The Fraction

The Communion

Hymn/Prayer

The Dismissal

The Lord's Prayer should be used in one or other of the places suggested on p. 29.